Copyright © **ticktock Entertainment Ltd 2006**
First published in Great Britain in 2006 by ticktock Media Ltd.,
Unit 2, Orchard Business Centre, North Farm Road, Tunbridge Wells, Kent TN2 3XF

ISBN 1 86007 855 9
Printed in China

Picture credits
t=top, b=bottom, c=centre, l=left, r=right
FLPA: 2, 4-5. 7c, 8-9c, 9tr, 10cl, 14l, 17c, 23c.
Every effort has been made to trace the copyright holders, and we apologise in advance for any unintentional omissions.
We would be pleased to insert the appropriate acknowledgements in any subsequent edition of this publication.

A CIP catalogue record for this book is available from the British Library.

contents

In the Jungle

There is so much to see in the jungle – from animals swinging through the vines to **fierce** creatures lurking in the **undergrowth**.

What can you see in the jungle?

Sloth

Toucan

Jaguar

Iguana

Tapir

Parrot

Monkey

Viper

Vines

Sloth

The sloth may be the laziest animal in the world. It moves very, very slowly and spends 20 hours a day just sleeping in tall trees.

The sloth stays still for so long that green **algae** grows in its hair.

The sloth has three claws on each limb. It hooks them around branches for a firm **grip.**

When the
sloth does move,
it has an **average** speed
of just two metres a minute.

The toucan is one of the easiest birds to **recognize** because of its **enormous bill**. It spends most of its time in high trees.

The toucan's yellow, black and red **plumage** helps it to recognize other toucans and find **mates**.

Its bill can be up to 20 centimetres long.

Toucans usually only fly over short distances. They weave up and down in the air a bit like a roller coaster.

The toucan uses its beak to reach into a tree and grab food.

 # Jaguar

The jaguar belongs to the cat family. Most have yellow **coats** covered in black rings, but black jaguars and white jaguars can also be seen.

The patterns on this jaguar's **coat** help it to blend in with its **surroundings**.

Each jaguar has slightly different markings. Jaguars live in the wild in southern USA and in South and Central America.

Jaguars can swim very well and sometimes catch fish to eat.

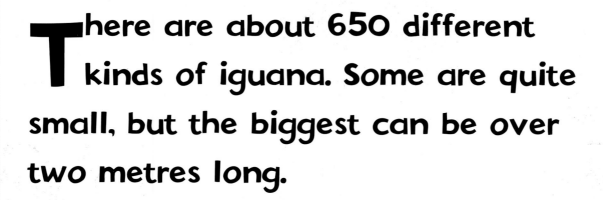

There are about 650 different kinds of iguana. Some are quite small, but the biggest can be over two metres long.

Young iguanas are very light green. This helps them to hide in the forest.

Iguanas are good climbers. Their long claws are good for **gripping** tree branches and vines.

An iguana spends a
lot of time **basking**
in the sun to
warm its body.

 # tapir

The tapir is a strange-looking animal with a large head.
Its nose is a bit like a short trunk.

Tapirs have
very poor eyesight.
They search for
food by smell.

Tapirs are good swimmers. If they are frightened, they dive into the water to hide.

Tapirs stay hidden from **predators** in the daytime. They come out at night to search for food.

The tapir has three toes on its back legs. It has four toes on its front legs.

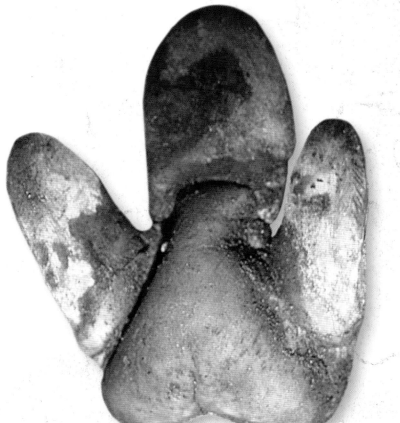

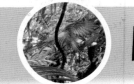 # parrot

These noisy birds have bright **plumage** and **powerful** beaks. They live high up in the branches of trees.

Parrots clean their feathers by pulling them carefully through their beaks, one at a time.

The parrot uses the hook at the top of its beak for scooping out the soft parts of fruit. The strong lower beak is good for opening seeds.

The parrot has very strong wings. It can fly very fast over short distances.

Monkey

There are many different kinds of monkey in the jungle. These monkeys are Golden Lion Tamarins. Monkeys are smaller than apes and gorillas, and they have tails.

Golden Lion Tamarins live in family groups. Both the father and mother help to look after babies.

Monkeys love to swing from branch to branch, high in the trees. Their long, slim fingers help them to hang on to branches.

Monkeys eat sweet fruit, insects and small lizards.

Monkeys can use their long tails like an extra hand.

 # Viper

Vipers are **poisonous** snakes. Their **fangs** fold up in their mouths and they swing downward when they want to bite something.

This Eyelash Viper has spiny scales above its eyes that look like eyelashes.

A pit between a viper's eyes can sense differences in heat. This helps the snake to track down its **prey.**

Vipers eat small **mammals**, lizards, frogs and birds. They come out to hunt at night.

There are more than 2,500 different kinds of vine in the jungle. Some types of vine, called lianas, can be as big as a person.

Vines grow **tendrils**, which wind around trees to provide support.

Some other types of vines, called strangler vines, grow so thick that they can kill the tree on which they are growing.

Vines spread quickly from one tree to another. They make up nearly half of the leaves in the rainforest **canopy**.

Glossary

Algae Very tiny plants

Average Usual or normal

Basking Lying in the sun

Bill Another name for a bird's beak

Canopy The highest part of the jungle, up in the treetops

Coat Name given to the fur of an animal

Enormous Very, very large

Fang A type of tooth that is sometmes hollow, so it can deliver poison as it bites

Fierce Violent and aggressive

Grip Holding on to with hands or feet

Mammal An animal that usually gives birth to live baby animals

Mate Animal partner of a different sex

Plumage The feathers of a bird

Poisonous Containing a substance that can cause death or illness

Powerful Very strong

Predator An animal that hunts down and kills other animals for food

Prey An animal that is hunted, killed and eaten by another animal

Recognize Know something by looking at different parts of it

Surroundings The area all around something

Tendrils Long, snakelike parts of a plant that can grab on to, wind around and hold things for support

Undergrowth The plants that grow under trees